SHAKE LOOSE MY SKIN

MY SKIN

NEW AND SELECTED POEMS

SONIA SANCHEZ

BEACON PRESS
BOSTON

BEACON PRESS
Boston, Massachusetts
www.beacon.org

BEACON PRESS BOOKS
are published under the auspices of
the Unitarian Universalist Association of Congregations.

20   24 23 22

This book is printed on acid-free paper that meets the uncoated paper
ANSI/NISO specifications for permanence as revised in 1992.

Text design by Anne Chalmers
Composition by Wilsted & Taylor Publishing Services

Library of Congress Cataloging-in-Publication Data

Sanchez, Sonia, 1935–
Shake loose my skin : new and selected poems / Sonia Sanchez.
p.   cm.
ISBN 978-0-8070-6853-3 (pbk.)
1. Afro-American women—Poetry.
2. Afro-Americans—Poetry.
I. Title.
PS3569.A468S53   1999
811'.54—dc21
98-41371

For Bernice and Adisa

CONTENTS

III. *from* Under a Soprano Sky 1987

IV. *from* Wounded in the House of a Friend 1995

V. *from* Does Your House Have Lions? 1997

from

I'VE BEEN A WOMAN
1978

Homecoming

i have been a
way so long
once after college
i returned tourist
style to watch all
the niggers killing
themselves with
three-for-oners
with
needles
that cd
not support
their stutters.
             now woman
i have returned
leaving behind me
all those hide and
seek faces peeling
with freudian dreams.
this is for real.
             black
             niggers
                  my beauty.
baby.
i have learned it
ain't like they say
in the newspapers.

Poem at Thirty

it is midnight
no magical bewitching
hour for me
i know only that
i am here waiting
remembering that
once as a child
i walked two
miles in my sleep.
did i know
then where i
was going?
traveling. i'm
always traveling.
i want to tell
you about me
about nights on a
brown couch when
i wrapped my
bones in lint and
refused to move.
no one touches
me anymore.
father do not
send me out
among strangers.
you you black man

stretching scraping
the mold from your body.
here is my hand.
i am not afraid
of the night.

Malcolm

do not speak to me of martydom
of men who die to be remembered
on some parish day.
i don't believe in dying
though i too shall die
and violets like castanets
will echo me.

yet this man
this dreamer,
thick-lipped with words
will never speak again
and in each winter
when the cold air cracks
with frost, i'll breathe
his breath and mourn
my gun-filled nights.
he was the sun that tagged
the western sky and
melted tiger-scholars
while they searched for stripes.
he said, "fuck you white
man. we have been
curled too long. nothing
is sacred now. not your
white face nor any
land that separates

until some voices
squat with spasms."

do not speak to me of living.
life is obscene with crowds
of white on black.
death is my pulse.
what might have been
is not for him/or me
but what could have been
floods the womb until i drown.

Personal Letter No. 2

i speak skimpily to
you about apartments i
no longer dwell in
and children who
chant their dis
obedience in choruses.
if i were young
i wd stretch you
with my wild words
while our nights
run soft with hands.
but i am what i
am. woman. alone
amid all this noise.

A Poem for My Father

how sad it must be
to love so many women
to need so many black
perfumed bodies weeping
underneath you.
        when i remember all those nights
i filled my mind with
long wars between short
sighted trojans & greeks
while you slapped some
wide hips about in
your pvt dungeon,
when i remember your
deformity   i want to
do something about your
makeshift manhood.
i guess
        that is why
on meeting your sixth
wife, i cross myself
with her confessionals.

Poem No. 3

i gather up
each sound
you left behind
and stretch them
on our bed.
          each nite
i breathe you
and become high.

Blues

in the night
in my half hour
negro dreams
i hear voices knocking at the door
i see walls dripping screams up
and down the halls
                    won't someone open
the door for me? won't some
one schedule my sleep
and don't ask no questions?
noise.
        like when he took me to his
home away from home place
and i died the long sought after
death he'd planned for me.
Yeah, bessie he put in the bacon
and it overflowed the pot.
and two days later
when i was talking
i started to grin.
as everyone knows
i am still grinning.

Haiku

did ya ever cry
Black man, did ya ever cry
til you knocked all over?

Sequences

1.

today I am
tired of sabbaths.
I seek a river of sticks
scratching the spine.
O I have laughed the clown's air
now my breath dries in paint.

2.

what is this profusion?
the sun does not burn
a cure, but hoards
while I stretch upward.
I hear, turning
in my shrug
a blaze of horns.
O I had forgotten parades
belabored with dreams.

3.

in my father's time
I fished in ponds
without fishes.

arching my throat,
I gargled amid nerves
and sang of redeemers.

> (o where have you been sweet
>> redeemer, sharp redeemer,
> o where have you been baroque
>> shimmer?
> i have been in coventry
> where ghosts danced in my veins
> i have heard you in all refrains.)

4.

ah the lull of
a yellow voice
that does not whine
with roots.
I have touched breasts
and buildings answered.
I have breathed
moth-shaped men
without seeds.
(O indiscriminate sleeves)

> (once upon an afternoon
> i became still-life

i carried a balloon
 and a long black knife.)

5.

love comes with pink eyes
with movements that run
green then blue again.
my thighs burn in crystal.

Haiku

if i had known, if
i had known you, i would have
left my love at home.

Poem No. 8

i've been a woman
  with my legs stretched by the wind
    rushing the day
      thinking i heard your voice
        while it was only the nite
          moving over
            making room for the dawn.

Present

1.

This woman vomiting her
hunger over the world
this melancholy woman forgotten
before memory came
this yellow movement bursting forth like
coltrane's melodies all mouth
buttocks moving like palm trees,
this honeycoatedalabamianwoman
raining rhythm of blue/black/smiles
this yellow woman carrying beneath her breasts
pleasures without tongues
this woman whose body weaves
desert patterns,
this woman, wet with wandering,
reviving the beauty of forests and winds
is telling you secrets
gather up your odors and listen
as she sings the mold from memory.

        there is no place
for a soft/black/woman.
there is no smile green enough or
summertime words warm enough to allow my growth.
and in my head
i see my history
standing like a shy child

and i chant lullabies
as i ride my past on horseback
tasting the thirst of yesterday tribes
hearing the ancient/black/woman
me, singing   hay-hay-hay-hay-ya-ya-ya.
                               hay-hay-hay-hay-ya-ha-ya.

like a slow scent
beneath the sun

        and i dance my
creation and my grandmothers gathering
from my bones like great wooden birds
spread their wings
while their long/legged/laughter
stretches the night.
        and i taste the
seasons of my birth. mangoes. papayas.
drink my woman/coconut/milks
stalk the ancient grandfathers
sipping on proud afternoons
walk with a song round my waist
tremble like a new/born/child troubled
with new breaths
        and my singing
becomes the only sound of a
blue/black/magical/woman. walking.
womb ripe. walking. loud with mornings. walking.
making pilgrimage to herself. walking.

Tanka

i kneel down like a
collector of jewels before
you. i am singing
one long necklace of love my
mouth a sapphire of grapes.

Tanka

autumn. a bonfire
of leaves. morning peels us toward
pomegranate festivals.
and in the evening i bring
you soup cooled by my laughter.

A Love Poem Written for Sterling Brown

(after reading a *New York Times* article re
a mummy kept preserved for about 3000 years)

I'm gonna get me some mummy tape for your love
preserve it for 3000 years or more
I'm gonna let the world see you
tapping a blue shell dance of love
I'm gonna ride your love bareback
on totem poles
bear your image on mountains
turning in ocean sleep
string your sighs thru the rainbow
of old age.
In the midst of desert people and times
I'm gonna fly your red/eagle/laughter 'cross the sky.

Kwa mama zetu waliotuzaa*

death is a five o'clock door forever changing time.
    and it was morning without sun or shadow;
a morning already afternoon. sky. cloudy with incense.
    and it was morning male in speech;
feminine in memory.
but i am speaking of everyday occurrences:
of days unrolling bandages for civilized wounds;
of gaudy women chanting rituals under a waterfall of stars;
of men freezing their sperms in diamond-studded wombs;
of children abandoned to a curfew of marble.

as morning is the same as nite death and life are one.
    spring. settling down on you like
green dust. mother. ambushed by pain in
rooms bloated with a century of cancer.
yo/face a scattered cry from queequeg's wooden bier.
    mother. i call out to you
traveling up the congo. i am preparing a place for you:
        nite made of female rain
        i am ready to sing her song
        prepare a place for her
        she comes to you out of turquoise pain.

        restring her eyes for me
        restring her body for me
        restring her peace for me

*for our mothers who gave us birth

23

no longer full of pain, may she walk
bright with orange smiles, may she walk
as it was long ago, may she walk

abundant with lightning steps, may she walk
abundant with green trails, may she walk
abundant with rainbows, may she walk
as it was long ago, may she walk

at the center of death is birth.
in those days when amherst fertilized by
black myths, rerouted the nile.
you became the word. (shirley, graham, du bois
                you were the dance
            pyramidal sister.
you told us in what egypt our feet
were chained
you. trained in the world's studio
painted the day with palaces
and before you marched the breath
of our ancestors.
                and yo/laughter passing
through a village of blacks
scattered the dead faces.
                and yo/voice lingering
like a shy goat fed our sad hungers.
and i. what pennsylvania day was i sucking dry

while you stuttering a thousand cries
hung yo/breasts on pagodas?
and i. what dreams had i suspended
above our short order lives
when death showered you with bells.
                    call her back for me
                    bells. call back this memory
                    still fresh with cactus pain.

                    call her name again. bells.
                    shirley. graham. du bois
                    has died in china
                    and her death demands a capsizing of tides.
olokun.*
                    she is passing yo/way while
                    pilgrim waves whistle complaints to man
olokun.
                    a bearer of roots is walking inside
                    of you.
                    prepare the morning nets to receive her.

before her peace, i know no thirst because of her
behind her peace, i know beauty because of her
under her peace, i know no fear because of her
over her peace, i am wealthy because of her

*Goddess of the sea

death is coming. the whole world hears
the buffalo walk of death passing thru the
archway of new life.

        the day is singing
        the day is singing
        he is singing in the mountains

        the nite is singing
        the nite is singing
        she is singing in the earth

i am circling new boundaries
i have been trailing the ornamental
songs of death (life
a strong pine tree
dancing in the wind

i inhale the ancient black breath
cry for every dying (living
creature

come. let us ascend from the
middle of our breath
sacred rhythms
inhaling peace.

from

HOMEGIRLS AND HANDGRENADES
1984

"Just Don't Never Give Up on Love"

Feeling tired that day, I came to the park with the children. I saw her as I rounded the corner, sitting old as stale beer on the bench, ruminating on some uneventful past. And I thought, "Hell. No rap from the roots today. I need the present. On this day. This Monday. This July day buckling me under her summer wings, I need more than old words for my body to squeeze into."

I sat down at the far end of the bench, draping my legs over the edge, baring my back to time and time unwell spent. I screamed to the children to watch those curves threatening their youth as they rode their 10-speed bikes against midwestern rhythms.

I opened my book and began to write. They were coming again, those words insistent as his hands had been, pounding inside me, demanding their time and place. I relaxed as my hands moved across the paper like one possessed.

I wasn't sure just what it was I heard. At first I thought it was one of the boys calling me so I kept on writing. They knew the routine by now. Emergencies demanded a presence. A facial confrontation. No long-distance screams across trees and space and other children's screams. But the sound pierced the pages and I looked around, and there she was inching her bamboo-creased body toward my back, coughing a beaded sentence off her tongue.

"Guess you think I ain't never loved, huh girl? Hee. Hee. Guess that what you be thinking, huh?"

I turned. Startled by her closeness and impropriety, I stuttered, "I, I, I, whhhaat dooooo you mean?"

"Hee. Hee. Guess you think I been old like this fo'ever, huh?" She leaned toward me, "Huh? I was so pretty that mens brought me breakfast in bed. Wouldn't let me hardly do no work at all."

"That's nice ma'am. I'm glad to hear that." I returned to my book. I didn't want to hear about some ancient love that she carried inside her. I had to finish a review for the journal. I was already late. I hoped she would get the hint and just sit still. I looked at her out of the corner of my eyes.

"He could barely keep hisself in changing clothes. But he was pretty. My first husband looked like the sun. I used to say his name over and over again 'til it hung from my ears like diamonds. Has you ever loved a pretty man, girl?"

I raised my eyes, determined to keep a distance from this woman disturbing my day.

"No ma'am. But I've seen many a pretty man. I don't like them though cuz they keep their love up high in a linen closet and I'm too short to reach it."

Her skin shook with laughter.

"Girl you gots some spunk about you after all. C'mon over here next to me. I wants to see yo' eyes up close. You looks so uneven sittin' over there."

Did she say uneven? Did this old buddha splintering death say uneven? Couldn't she see that I had one eye shorter than the other; that my breath was painted on porcelain; that one breast crocheted keloids under this white blouse?

I moved toward her though. I scooped up the years that had stripped me to the waist and moved toward her. And she called to me to come out, come out wherever you are young woman, playing hide and go seek with scarecrow men. I gathered myself up at the gateway of her confessionals.

"Do you know what it mean to love a pretty man, girl?" She crooned in my ear. "You always running behind a man like that girl while he cradles his privates. Ain't no joy in a pretty yellow man, cuz he always out pleasurin' and givin' pleasure."

I nodded my head as her words sailed in my ears. Here was the pulse of a woman whose black ass shook the world once.

She continued. "A woman crying all the time is pitiful. Pitiful I says. I wuz pitiful sitting by the window every night like a cow in the fields chewin' on cud. I wanted to cry out, but not even God hisself could hear me. I tried to cry out til my mouth wuz split open at the throat. I 'spoze there is a time all womens has to visit the slaughter house. My visit lasted five years."

Touching her hands, I felt the summer splintering in prayer; touching her hands, I felt my bones migrating in red noise. I asked, "When did you see the butterflies again?"

Her eyes wandered like quicksand over my face. Then she smiled, "Girl don't you know yet that you don't never give up on love? Don't you know you has in you the pulse of winds? The noise of dragonflies?" Her eyes squinted close and she said, "One of them mornings he woke up callin' me and I wuz gone. I wuz gone running with the moon over my shoulders. I looked no which way at all. I had inside me 'nough knives and spoons to cut/scoop out the night. I wuz a-tremblin' as I met the mornin'."

She stirred in her 84-year-old memory. She stirred up her body as she talked. "They's men and mens. Some good. Some bad. Some breathing death. Some breathing life. William wuz my beginnin'. I come to my second husband spittin' metal and he just pick me up and fold me inside him. I wuz christen' with his love."

She began to hum. I didn't recognize the song; it was a prayer. I leaned back and listened to her voice rustling like silk. I heard cathedrals and sonnets; I heard tents and revivals and a black woman spilling black juice among her ruins.

"We all gotta salute death one time or 'nother girl. Death be waitin' outdoors trying to get inside. William died at his job. Death just turned 'round and snatched him right off the street."

Her humming became the only sound in the park. Her voice moved across the bench like a mutilated child. And I cried. For myself. For this woman talkin' about love. For all the women who have ever stretched their bodies out anticipating civilization and finding ruins.

The crashing of the bikes was anticlimactic. I jumped

up, rushed toward the accident. Man. Little man. Where you bicycling to so very fast? Man. Second little man. Take it slow. It all passes so fast anyhow.

As I walked the boys and their bikes toward the bench, I smiled at this old woman waiting for our return.

"I want you to meet a great lady, boys."

"Is she a writer, too, ma?"

"No honey. She's a lady who has lived life instead of writing about it."

"After we say hello can we ride a little while longer? Please!"

"Ok. But watch your manners now and your bones afterwards."

"These are my sons, Ma'am."

"How you do sons? I'm Mrs. Rosalie Johnson. Glad to meet you."

The boys shook her hand and listened for a minute to her words. Then they rode off, spinning their wheels on a city neutral with pain.

As I stood watching them race the morning, Mrs. Johnson got up.

"Don't go," I cried. "You didn't finish your story."

"We'll talk by-and-by. I comes out here almost every day. I sits here on the same bench every day. I'll probably die sittin' here one day. As good a place as any I 'magine."

"May I hug you ma'am? You've helped me so much today. You've given me strength to keep on looking."

"No. Don't never go looking for love girl. Just wait. It'll come. Like the rain fallin' from the heaven, it'll come. Just don't never give up on love."

We hugged; then she walked her 84-year-old walk down the street. A black woman. Echoing gold. Carrying couplets from the sky to crease the ground.

Ballad

(after the Spanish)

forgive me if i laugh
you are so sure of love
you are so young
and i too old to learn of love.

the rain exploding
in the air is love
the grass excreting her
green wax is love
and stones remembering
past steps is love,
but you. you are too young
for love
and i too old.

once. what does it matter
when or who, i knew
of love.
i fixed my body
under his and went
to sleep in love
all trace of me
was wiped away

forgive me if i smile
young heiress of a naked dream
you are so young
and i too old to learn to love.

After Saturday Night Comes Sunday

It had all started at the bank. She wuzn't sure, but she thot it had. At that crowded bank where she had gone to clear up the mistaken notion that she wuz $300.00 overdrawn in her checking account.

Sandy had moved into that undersized/low expectation of niggahs/being able to save anything bank/meanly. She wuz tired of people charging her fo they own mistakes. She had seen it wid her own eyes, five checks: four fo $50 the other one fo $100 made out to an Anthony Smith. It wuz Winston's signature. Her stomach jumped as she added and re-added the figures. Finally she dropped the pen and looked up at the business/suited/man sitten across from her wid crossed legs and eyes. And as she called him faggot in her mind, watermelon tears gathered round her big eyes and she just sat.

Someone had come for her at the bank. A friend of Winston's helped her to his car. It wuz the wite/dude who followed Winston constantly wid his eyes. Begging eyes she had once called em, half in jest, half seriously. They wuz begging now, along wid his mouth, begging Sandy to talk. But she cudn't. The words had gone away, gotten lost, drowned by the warm/april/rain dropping in on her as she watched the car move down the long/unbending/street. It was her first Spring in Indianapolis. She wondered if it wud be beautiful.

He wuz holding her. Crying in her ear. Loud cries, almost louder than the noise already turning in her head. Yeh. He sed between the cries that he had messed up the money. He had . . . he had . . . oh babee. *C'mon Sandy and talk. Talk to me. Help me, babee. Help me to tell you what I got to tell you for both our sakes.* He stretched her out on the green/over-sized/couch that sat out from the wall like some displaced trailer waiting to be parked.

I'm hooked, he sed. I'm hooked again on stuff. It's not like befo though when I wuz 17 and just beginning. This time it's different. I mean it has to do now wid me and all my friends who are still on junk. You see I got out of the joint and looked around and saw those brothers who are my friends all still on the stuff and I cried inside. I cried long tears for some beautiful dudes who didn't know how the man had 'em by they balls. Baby I felt so sorry for them and they wuz so turned around that one day over to Tony's crib I got high wid 'em. That's all babee. I know I shouldn't have done that. You and the kids and all. But they wuz dudes I wuz in the joint wid. My brothers who wuz still unaware. I can git clean, babee. I mean, I don't have a long jones. I ain't been on it too long. I can kick now. Tomorrow. You just say it. Give me the word/ sign that you understand, forgive me for being one big ass-hole and I'll start kicking tomorrow. For you babee. I know I been laying some heavy stuff on you. Spending money we ain't even got—I'll git a job too next week—staying out all the time. Hitting you fo telling me the truth 'bout myself. My actions. Babee, it's you I love in spite of my crazy actions. It's you I love. Don't nobody else mean to me what you do. It's just that I been acting crazy but I know I can't keep on keepin' on this way and keep you and the children. Give me a whole lot of slack during this time and I can kick it, babee. I love you. You so good to me. The meanest thing that done ever happened to me. You the best thing that ever happened to me in all of my 38 years and I'll take better care of you. Say something Sandy. Say you understand it all. Say you forgive me. At least that, babee.

He raised her head from the couch and kissed her. It was a short cooling kiss. Not warm. Not long. A binding kiss. She opened her eyes and looked at him, and the bare room that somehow now complemented their lives, and she started to cry again. And as he grabbed her and rocked her, she spoke fo the first time since she had told that wite/collar/man in the bank that the bank was wrong.

The-the-the-the bab-bab-bab-ies. Ar-ar-ar-are th-th-th-they o-o-okay? Oh my god. I'm stuttering. Stuttering, she thot. Just like when I wuz little. Stop talking. Stop talking girl. Write what you have to say. Just like you used to when you wuz little and you got tired of people staring at you while you pushed words out of an unaccommodating mouth. Yeh. That was it, she thot. Stop talking and write what you have to say. Nod yo/head to all of this madness. But rest yo/head and use yo/hands till you git it all straight again.

She pointed to her bag and he handed it to her. She took out a pen and notebook and wrote that she wuz tired, that her head hurt and wuz spinning, and that she wanted to sleep fo awhile. She turned and held his face full of little sores where he had picked fo ingrown hairs the nite befo. She kissed them and let her tongue move over his lips, wetting them. He smiled at her and sed he wud git her a coupla sleeping pills. He wud also pick up some dollies fo himself cuz Saturday was kicking time fo him. As he went out the door he turned and sed, *Lady, you some lady. I'm a lucky M.F. to have found you.* She watched him from the window and the sun hit the gold of his dashiki and made it bleed yellow raindrops.

She must have dozed. She knew it wuz late. It was dark outside. The room was dark also and she wondered if he had come in and gone upstairs where the children were napping. What a long nap the boys were taking. They wud be up all nite tonite if they didn't wake up soon. Maybe she shud wake them up, but she decided against it. Her body wuz still tired and she heard footsteps on the porch.

His voice was light and cracked a little as he explained his delay. He wuz high. She knew it. He sounded like he sounded on the phone when he called her late in the nite from some loud place and complimented her fo understanding his late hours. She hadn't understood them, she just hated to be a complaining bitch. He had no sleeping pills, but he had gotten her something as good. A morphine tablet. She watched his face as he explained that she cud swallow it or pop it into the skin. He sed it worked better if you stuck it in yo/arm. As he took the tablet out of the cellophane paper of his cigarettes, she closed her eyes and fo a moment, she thot she heard someone crying outside the house. She opened her eyes.

His body hung loose as he knelt by the couch. He took from his pocket a manila envelope. It had little spots of blood on it and as he undid the rubber hands, she saw two needles, a black top wid two pieces of dirty, wite cotton balls in it. She knew this wuz what he used to git high wid.

I-I-I-I-I don-don-don-don't wa-wa-want none o-o-o-of that stuff, ma-a-a-a-a-n. Ain't th-th-th-that do-do-do-dope, too? I-I-I-I-I just just just just wa-wa-wa-nnnt-ted to sleep. I'm o-o-o-kay now. She picked up her notebook and pen and started to write again.

I slept while you wuz gone, man. I drifted on off as I looked for you to walk up the steps. I don't want that stuff. Give me a cold beer though, if there's any in the house. I'll drink that. But no stuff man, she wrote. I'm yo/woman. You shudn't be giving me any of that stuff. Throw the pill away. We don't need it. You don't need it any mo. You gon kick and we gon move on. Keep on being baddDDD togetha. I'll help you, man, cuz I know you want to kick. Flush it down the toilet! You'll start kicking tomorrow and I'll get a babysitter and take us fo a long drive in the country and we'll move on the grass and make it move wid us, cuz we'll be full of living/

*alive/thots and we'll stop and make love in the middle of no-
where, and the grass will stop its wintry/brown/chants and
become green as our Black bodies sing. Heave. Love each
other. Throw that stuff away, man, cuz we got more impor-
tant/beautiful/things to do.*

As he read the note his eyes looked at hers in a half/clear/
way and he got up and walked slowly to the john. She heard
the toilet flushing and she heard the refrigerator door open
and close. He brought two cold beers and, as she opened
hers, she sat up to watch him rock back and forth in the
rocking chair. And his eyes became small and sad as he sed,
half jokingly, *Hope I don't regret throwing that stuff in the
toilet,* and he leaned back and smiled sadly as he drank his
beer. She turned the beer can up to her lips and let the cold
evening foam wet her mouth and drown the gathering stut-
ters of her mind.

The sound of cries from the second floor made her move.
As she climbed the stairs she waved to him. But his eyes
were still closed. He wuz somewhere else, not in this house
she thot. He wuz somewhere else, floating among past
dreams she had never seen or heard him talk about. As she
climbed the stairs, the boys' screams grew louder. *Wow.
Them boys got some strong lungs,* she thot. And smiled.

It wuz 11:30 and she had just put the boys in their cribs.
She heard them sucking on their bottles, working hard at
nourishing themselves. She knew the youngest twin wud

finish his bottle first and cry out fo more milk befo he slept. She laughed out loud. He sho cud grease.

He wuz in the bathroom. She knocked on the door, but he sed for her not to come in. She stood outside the door, not moving, and knocked again. *Go and turn on the TV*, he sed, *I'll be out in a few minutes.*

It wuz 30 minutes later when he came out. His walk wuz much faster than befo and his voice wuz high, higher than the fear moving over her body. She ran to him, threw her body against him and held on. She kissed him hard and moved her body 'gainst him til he stopped and paid attention to her movements. They fell to the floor. She felt his weight on her as she moved and kissed him. She wuz feeling good and she cudn't understand why he stopped. In the midst of pulling off her dress he stopped and took out a cigarette and lit it while she undressed to her bra and panties. She felt naked all of a sudden and sat down and drew her legs up against her chest and closed her eyes. She reached for a cigarette and lit it.

He stretched out next to her. She felt very ashamed, as if she had made him do something wrong. She wuz glad that she cudn't talk cuz that way she didn't have to explain. He ran his hand up and down her legs and touched her soft wet places.

It's just, babee, that this stuff kills any desire for THAT! I mean, I want you and all that but I can't quite git it up to per-

form. He lit another cigarette and sat up. *Babee, you sho know how to pick 'em. I mean, wuz you born under an unlucky star or sumthin'? First, you had a nigguh who preferred a rich/wite/woman to you and Blackness. Now you have a junkie who can't even satisfy you when you need satisfying.* And his laugh wuz harsh as he sed again, *You sho know how to pick 'em, lady.* She didn't know what else to do so she smiled a nervous smile that made her feel, remember times when she wuz little and she had stuttered thru a sentence and the listener had acknowledged her accomplishment wid a smile and all she cud do was smile back.

He turned and held her and sed, *Stay up wid me tonite, babee. I got all these memories creeping in on me. Bad ones. They's the things that make kicking hard, you know. You begin remembering all the mean things you've done to yo/family/friends who dig you. I'm remembering now all the heavee things I done laid on you in such a short time. You hardly had a chance to catch yo/breath when I'd think of sum new game to lay on you. Help me, Sandy. Listen to my talk. Hold my hand when I git too sad. Laugh at my fears that keep poppin' out on me like some childhood disease. Be my vaccine, babee. I need you. Don't ever leave me, babee, cuz I'll never have a love like you again. I'll never have another woman again if you leave me.* He picked up her hands and rubbed them in his palms as he talked, and she listened until he finally slept and morning crept in through the shades and covered them.

He threw away his works when he woke up. He came over to where she wuz feeding the boys and kissed her and walked out to the backyard and threw the manila envelope into the middle can. He came back inside, smiled and took a dollie wid a glass of water, and fell on the couch.

Sandy put the boys in their strollers in the backyard where she cud watch them as she cleaned the kitchen. She saw Snow, their big/wite/dog, come round the corner of the house to sit in front of them. They babbled words to him but he sat still guarding them from the backyard/evils of the world.

She moved fast in the house, had a second cup of coffee, called their babysitter and finished straightening up the house. She put on a short dress which showed her legs, and she felt good about her black/hairy legs. She laughed as she remembered that the young brothers on her block used to call her a big/legged/momma as she walked in her young ways.

They never made the country. Their car refused to start and Winston wuz too sick to push it to the filling station for a jump. So they walked to the park. He pushed her in the swing and she pumped herself higher and higher and higher till he told her to stop. She let the swing come slowly to a stop and she jumped out and hit him on the behind and ran. She heard him gaining on her and she tried to dodge him but they fell laughing and holding each other. She looked at him and her eyes sed, *I wish you cud make love to me man.* As she laughed and pushed him away she thot, *but just you wait til you all right Winston, I'll give you a workout you'll never forget,* and they got up and walked till he felt bad and went home.

He stayed upstairs while she cooked. When she went upstairs to check on him, he was curled up, wrapped tight as a child in his mother's womb. She wiped his head and body full of sweat and kissed him and thought how beautiful he wuz and how proud she wuz of him. She massaged his back and went away. He called fo her as she wuz feeding the children and asked for the wine. He needed somethin' else to relieve this saturday/nite/pain that was creeping up on him. He looked bad, she thot, and raced down the stairs and brought him the sherry. He thanked her as she went out the door and she curtsied, smiled and sed, *Any ol time, man.* She noticed she hadn't stuttered and felt good.

By the time she got back upstairs he was moaning and turning back and forth on the bed. He had drunk half the wine in the bottle, now he wuz getting up to bring it all up. When she came back up to the room he sed he was cold, so she got another blanket for him. He wuz still cold, so she took off her clothes and got under the covers wid him and rubbed her body against him. She wuz scared. She started to sing a Billie Holiday song. Yeh. God bless the child that's got his own. She cried in between the lyrics as she felt his big frame trembling and heaving. *Oh god,* she thot, *am I doing the right thing?* He soon quieted down and got up to go to the toilet. She closed her eyes as she waited fo him. She closed her eyes and felt the warmth of the covers creeping over her. She remembered calling his name as she drifted off to sleep. She remembered how quiet everything finally wuz.

One of the babies woke her up. She went into the room, picked up his bottle and got him more milk. It wuz while she wuz handing him the milk that she heard the silence. She ran to their bedroom and turned on the light. The bed wuz empty. She ran down the stairs and turned on the lights. He was gone. She saw her purse on the couch. Her wallet wuz empty. Nothing was left. She opened the door and went out on the porch, and she remembered the lights were on and that she wuz naked. But she stood fo a moment looking out at the flat/Indianapolis/street and she stood and let the late/nite/air touch her body and she turned and went inside.

I Have Walked a Long Time

i have walked a long time
much longer than death that splinters
wid her innuendos.
my life, ah my alien life,
is like an echo of nostalgia
bringen blue screens to bury clouds
rinsen wite stones stretched among the sea.

> you, man, will you remember me when i die?
> will you stare and stain my death and say
> i saw her dancen among swallows
> far from the world's obscenities?
> you, man, will you remember and cry?

and i have not loved.
always
while the body prowls
the soul catalogues each step;
while the unconscious unbridles feasts
the flesh knots toward the shore.
ah, i have not loved
wid legs stretched like stalks against sheets
wid stomachs drainen the piracy of oceans
wid mouths discarden the gelatin
to shake the sharp self.
i have walked by memory of others
between the blood night

and twilights
i have lived in tunnels
and fed the bloodless fish;
between the yellow rain
and ash,
i have heard the rattle
of my seed,
so time, like some pearl necklace embracen
a superior whore, converges
and the swift spider binds my breast.

you, man, will you remember me when i die?
will you stare and stain my death and say
i saw her applauden suns
far from the grandiose audience?
you, man, will you remember and cry?

On Passing thru Morgantown, Pa.

i saw you
vincent van
gogh perched
on those pennsylvania
cornfields communing
amid secret black
bird societies. yes.
i'm sure that was
you exploding your
fantastic delirium
while in the
distance
red indian
hills beckoned.

On Seeing a Pacifist Burn

this day is not
real. the crowing of
the far-away
carillons ring
out direction
less. even you are
un real roasting
under a man
hattan sky
while passersby flap
their indecent tongues.
even i am un
real but i
am black and
thought to be
without meaning.

Letter to Ezekiel Mphahlele

dear zeke,

i've just left your house where you and rebecca served a dinner of peace to me and my sons. the ride home is not as long as the way i came, two centuries of hunger brought me along many detours before i recognized your house. it is raining and as i watch the raindrops spin like colored beads on the windshield, i hear your voice calling out to your ancestors to prepare a place for you, for you were returning home leaving the skeleton rites of twenty years behind.

you and rebecca have been walking a long time. your feet have crossed the african continent to this western one where you moved amid leaden eyes and laughter that froze you in snow/capped memories. your journey began in 1957, when the ruling class could not understand your yawns of freedom, the motion of a million eyes to see for themselves what life was/is and could be, and you cut across the burial grounds of south africa where many of your comrades slept and you cut across those black africans smiling their long smiles from diplomatic teeth. now you are returning home. now your mother's womb cries out to you. now your history demands your heartbeat. and you turn your body toward the whirlwind of change, toward young black voices calling for a dignity speeding beyond control, on the right side of the road. but this nite full of whispering summer trees, this nite nodding with south african faces, heard you say, sonia. i must be buried in my country in my own homeland, my bones must replenish the black earth from whence they came, our bones must fertilize the ground on which we walk or we shall never walk as men and women in the 21st century.

i talked to my sons as the car chased the longlegged rain running before us. i told them that men and women are measured by their acts not by their swaggering speech or walk, or the money they have stashed between their legs. i talked to my sons about bravery outside of bruce lee grunts and jabs, outside of star wars' knights fertilizing america's green youth into continued fantasies while reality explodes in neutron boldness. i said you have just sat and eaten amid bravery. relish the taste. stir it around and around in your mouth until the quick sweetness of it becomes bitter, then swallow it slowly, letting this new astringent taste burn the throat. bravery is no easy taste to swallow. i said this man and woman we have just left this nite have decided to walk like panthers in their country, to breathe again their own breath suspended by twenty years of exile, to settle in the maternal space of their birth where there are men who "shake hands without hearts" waiting for them. they are a fixed portrait of courage.

it is 2 a.m., my children stretch themselves in dreams, kicking away the room's shadows. i stare at the nite piling in little heaps near my bed. zeke. maybe you are a madman. i a madwoman to want to walk across the sea, to saddle time while singing a future note. we follow the new day's breath, we answer old bruises waiting to descend upon our heads, we answer screams creeping out of holes and shells buried by memories waiting to be cleansed. you invoking the ghosts lurking inside this child/woman. you breaking my curtain of silence. i love the tom-tom days you are marching, your feet rooted in the sea. save a space for me and mine zeke and rebecca. this lost woman, who walks her own shadow for peace.

from

UNDER
A SOPRANO
SKY
1987

Under a Soprano Sky

1.

once i lived on pillars in a green house
boarded by lilacs that rocked voices into weeds.
i bled an owl's blood
shredding the grass until i
rocked in a choir of worms.
obscene with hands, i wooed the world
with thumbs
                while yo-yos hummed.
was it an unborn lacquer i peeled?
the woods, tall as waves, sang in mixed
tongues that loosened the scalp
and my bones wrapped in white dust
returned to echo in my thighs.

i heard a pulse wandering somewhere
on vague embankments.
O are my hands breathing? I cannot smell the nerves.
i saw the sun
ripening green stones for fields.
O have my eyes run down? i cannot taste my birth.

2.

now as i move, mouth quivering with silks
my skin runs soft with eyes.

descending into my legs, i follow obscure birds
purchasing orthopedic wings.
the air is late this summer.

i peel the spine and flood
the earth with adolescence.
O who will pump these breasts? I cannot waltz my tongue.

under a soprano sky, a woman sings,
lovely as chandeliers.

Philadelphia: Spring, 1985

1.

*/a phila. fireman reflects after
seeing a decapitated body in the MOVE ruins/*

to see those eyes
orange like butterflies
over the walls.

i must move away
from this little-ease
where the pulse
shrinks into itself
and carve myself in white.

O to press the seasons
and taste the quiet juice
of their veins.

2. */memory/*

a.

Thus in the varicose town
where eyes splintered the night with glass

the children touched at random
sat in places where legions rode.

And O we watched the young birds
stretch the sky
until it streamed white ashes
and O we saw mountains lean on seas
to drink the blood of whales
then wander dumb with their wet bowels.

b.

Everywhere young
faces breathing in crusts.
breakfast of dreams.
The city, lit by a single fire,
followed the air into disorder.
And the sabbath stones singed our eyes
with each morning's coin.

c.

Praise of a cureless death they heard
without confessor;
Praise of cathedrals
pressing their genesis from priests;
Praise of wild gulls who came and drank

their summer's milk,
then led them toward the parish snow.

How still the spiderless city.
The earth is immemorial in death.

Haiku

(for the police on Osage Ave.)

they came eating their
own mouths orgiastic teeth
smiling crucifixions

Dear Mama,

It is Christmas eve and the year is passing away with cal-
loused feet. My father, your son and I decorate the night
with words. Sit ceremoniously in human song. Watch our
blue sapphire words eclipse the night. We have come to this
simplicity from afar.

He stirs, pulls from his pocket a faded picture of you.
Blackwoman. Sitting in frigid peace. All of your biography
preserved in your face. And my eyes draw up short as he
says, "Her name was Elizabeth but we used to call her Liz-
zie." And I hold your picture in my hands. But I know your
name by heart. It's Mama. I hold you in my hands and let
time pass over my face: "Let my baby be. She ain't like the
others. She rough. She'll stumble on gentleness later on."

Ah Mama. Gentleness ain't never been no stranger to my
genes. But I did like the roughness of running and swal-
lowing the wind, diving in rivers I could barely swim, jump-
ing from second story windows into a saving backyard
bush. I did love you for loving me so hard until I slid inside
your veins and sailed your blood to an uncrucified shore.

And I remember Saturday afternoons at our house. The
old sister deaconesses sitting in sacred pain. Black cadav-
ers burning with lost aromas. And I crawled behind the
couch and listened to breaths I had never breathed. Tasted
their enormous martyrdom. Lives spent on so many things.
Heard their laughter at Sister Smith's latest performance in
church—her purse sailing toward Brother Thomas's head

again. And I hugged the laughter round my knees. Draped it round my shoulder like a Spanish shawl.

And history began once again. I received it and let it circulate in my blood. I learned on those Saturday afternoons about women rooted in themselves, raising themselves in dark America, discharging their pain without ever stopping. I learned about women fighting men back when they hit them: "Don't never let no mens hit you mo than once girl." I learned about "womens waking up they mens" in the nite with pans of hot grease and the compromises reached after the smell of hot grease had penetrated their sleepy brains. I learned about loose women walking their abandoned walk down front in church, crossing their legs instead of their hands to God. And I crept into my eyes. Alone with my daydreams of being woman. Adult. Powerful. Loving. Like them. Allowing nobody to rule me if I didn't want to be.

And when they left. When those old bodies had gathered up their sovereign smells. After they had kissed and packed up beans snapped and cakes cooked and laughter bagged. After they had called out their last goodbyes, I crawled out of my place. Surveyed the room. Then walked over to the couch where some had sat for hours and bent my head and smelled their evening smells. I screamed out loud, "Oooweeee! Ain't that stinky!" and I laughed laughter from a thousand corridors. And you turned Mama, closed the door, chased me round the room until I crawled into a corner where your large body could not reach me. But your laughter pierced the little alcove where I sat laughing at the night. And your humming sprinkled my small space. Your humming about your Jesus and how one day he was gonna take you home . . .

Because you died when I was six Mama, I never laughed like that again. Because you died without warning Mama, my sister and I moved from family to stepmother to friend of the family. I never felt your warmth again.

But I knew corners and alcoves and closets where I was pushed when some mad woman went out of control. Where I sat for days while some woman raved in rhymes about unwanted children. And work. And not enough money. Or love. And I sat out my childhood with stutters and poems gathered in my head like some winter storm. And the poems erased the stutters and pain. And the words loved me and I loved them in return.

My first real poem was about you Mama and death. My first real poem recited an alphabet of spit splattering a white bus driver's face after he tried to push cousin Lucille off a bus and she left Birmingham under the cover of darkness. Forever. My first real poem was about your Charles-white arms holding me up against death.

My life flows from you Mama. My style comes from a long line of Louises who picked me up in the nite to keep me from wetting the bed. A long line of Sarahs who fed me and my sister and fourteen other children from watery soups and beans and a lot of imagination. A long line of Lizzies who made me understand love. Sharing. Holding a child up to the stars. Holding your tribe in a grip of love. A long line of Black people holding each other up against silence.

I still hear your humming Mama. The color of your song calls me home. The color of your words saying, "Let her be. She got a right to be different. She gonna stumble on herself one of these days. Just let the child be."

And I be Mama.

Fall

i have been drunk since
summer, sure you would
come to sift the waves
until they flaked like
diamonds over our flanks.
i have not moved
even when wild
horses, with snouts like pigs
came to violate me,
i squatted in
my baptism.
O hear the sea
galloping like stallions
toward spring.

Fragment 1

alone
deranged by loitering
i hear the bricks pacing my window.
my pores know how to come.
what survives in me
i still suspect.

how still this savior.
white suit in singing hand.
spitting mildew air.
who shapes the shade
is.

i am a reluctant ache
authenticating my bones.
i shall spread out my veins
and beat the dust into noise.

Fragment 2

I am reciting the rain
caught in my scream.
these lips cannot swim
only by breasts wild as
black waves.

I met a collector of rain   once
who went to sleep in my sleeve.
is his alibi still under
my arm?

I keep coughing up butterflies
my entrails trail albino tunes
his voice comes in my hair.
is the flesh tender where the knees weep?

Haiku

man. you write me so
much you bad as the loanhouse
asking fo they money

Towhomitmayconcern

watch out fo the full moon of sonia
shinin down on ya.
git yo/self fattened up man
you gon be doing battle with me
ima gonna stake you out
grind you down
leave greasy spots all over yo/soul
till you bone dry. man.
you gon know you done been touched by me
this time.
ima gonna tattoo me on you fo ever
leave my creases all inside yo creases
i done warned ya boy
watch out
for the full moon of sonia
shinin down on ya.

Blues

will you love me baby when the sun goes down
i say will you love me baby when the sun goes down
or you just a summertime man leaving fo winter comes round.

will you keep me baby when i'm feeling down 'n' out
i say will you hold me baby when i'm feeling down 'n' out
or will you just stop & spit while i lives from hand to mouth.

done drunk so much of you i staggers in my sleep
i say done drunk so much of you man, i staggers in my sleep
when i wakes up baby, gonna start me on a brand new week.

will you love me baby when the sun goes down
i say will you love me baby when the sun goes down
or you just a summertime man leaving fo winter comes round.

Song No. 2

(1)

i say. all you young girls waiting to live
i say. all you young girls taking yo pill
i say. all you sisters tired of standing still
i say. all you sisters thinkin you won't, but you will.

don't let them kill you with their stare
don't let them closet you with no air
don't let them feed you sex piecemeal
don't let them offer you any old deal.

i say. step back sisters. we're rising from the dead
i say. step back johnnies. we're dancing on our heads
i say. step back man. no mo hangin by a thread
i say. step back world. can't let it all go unsaid.

(2)

i say. all you young girls molested at ten
i say. all you young girls giving it up again & again
i say. all you sisters hanging out in every den
i say. all you sisters needing your own oxygen.

don't let them trap you with their coke
don't let them treat you like one fat joke

don't let them bleed you till you broke
don't let them blind you in masculine smoke.

i say. step back sisters. we're rising from the dead
i say. step back johnnies. we're dancing on our heads
i say. step back man. no mo hanging by a thread.
i say. step back world. can't let it go unsaid.

An Anthem

(for the ANC and Brandywine Peace Community)

Our vision is our voice
we cut through the country
where madmen goosestep in tune to Guernica.

we are people made of fire
we walk with ceremonial breaths
we have condemned talking mouths.

we run without legs
we see without eyes
loud laughter breaks over our heads.

give me courage so I can spread
it over my face and mouth.

we are secret rivers
with shaking hips and crests
come awake in our thunder
so that our eyes can see behind trees.

for the world is split wide open
and you hide your hands behind your backs
for the world is broken into little pieces
and you beg with tin cups for life.

are we not more than hunger and music?
are we not more than harlequins and horns?

are we not more than color and drums?
are we not more than anger and dance?

give me courage so I can spread it
over my face and mouth.

we are the shakers
walking from top to bottom in a day
we are like Shango
involving ourselves in acts
that bring life to the middle
of our stomachs

we are coming towards you madmen
shredding your death talk
standing in front with mornings around our waist
we have inherited our prayers from
the rain
our eyes from the children of Soweto.

red rain pours over the land
and our fire mixes with the water.

give me courage so I can spread
it over my face and mouth.

Graduation Notes

(for Mungu, Morani, Monica, and Andrew and Crefeld seniors)

So much of growing up is an unbearable waiting. A constant longing for another time. Another season.

I remember walking like you today down this path. In love with the day. Flesh awkward. I sang at the edge of adolescence and the scent of adulthood rushed me and I thought I would suffocate. But I didn't. I am here. So are you. Finally. Tired of tiny noises your eyes hum a large vibration.

I think all journeys are the same. My breath delighting in the single dawn. Yours. Walking at the edge. Unafraid. Anxious for the unseen dawns are mixing today like the underground rhythms seeping from your pores.

At this moment your skins living your eighteen years suspend all noises. Your days still half-opened, crackle like the fires to come. Outside. The earth. Wind. Night. Unfold for you. Listen to their sounds. They have sung me seasons that never abandoned me. A dance of summer rain. A ceremony of thunder waking up the earth to human monuments.

Facing each other I smile at your faces. Know you as young heroes soon to be decorated with years. Hope no wars dwarf you. Know your dreams wild and sweet will sail from your waists to surround the non-lovers. Dreamers. And you will rise up like newborn armies refashioning lives. Louder than the sea you come from.

IV

from

WOUNDED IN THE HOUSE OF A FRIEND
1995

Wounded in the House of a Friend

Set No. 1

the unspoken word
is born, i see it in our
eyes dancing

She hadn't found anything. i had been careful. No lipstick.
No matches from a well-known bar. No letters. Cards.
Confessing an undying love. Nothing tangible for her to
hold onto. But i knew she knew. It had been on her face, in
her eyes for the last nine days. It was the way she looked at
me sideways from across the restaurant table as she picked
at her brown rice sushi. It was the way she paused in profile
while inspecting my wolfdreams. It was the way her mouth
took a detour from talk. And then as we exited the restau-
rant she said it quite casually: i know there's another
woman. You must tell me about her when we get home.

Yeah. There was another woman. In fact there were
three women. In Florida, California, and North Carolina.
Places to replace her cool detachment of these last years.
No sex for months. Always tired or sick or off to some con-
ference designed to save the world from racism or extinc-
tion. If i had jerked off one more time in bed while lying
next to her it woulda dropped off. Still i wondered how she
knew.

am i dressed right for the smoke?
will it wrinkle if i fall?

i had first felt something was wrong at the dinner party. His colleague's house. He was so animated. The first flush of his new job i thought. He spoke staccato style. Two drinks in each hand. His laughter. Wild. Hard. Contagious as shrines enveloped the room. He was so wired that i thought he was going to explode. i didn't know the people there. They were all lawyers. Even the wives were lawyers. Glib and self-assured. Discussing cases, and colleagues. Then it happened. A small hesitation on his part. In answer to a question as to how he would be able to get some important document from one place to another, he looked at the host and said: They'll get it to me. Don't worry. And the look passing back and forth between the men told of collusion and omission. Told of dependence on other women for information and confirmation. Told of nites i had stretched out next to him and he was soft. Too soft for my open legs. And i turned my back to him and the nites multiplied out loud. As i drove home from the party i asked him what was wrong? What was bothering him? Were we okay? Would we make love tonite? Would we ever make love again? Did my breath stink? Was i too short? Too tall? Did i talk too much? Should i wear lipstick? Should i cut my hair? Let it grow? What did he want for dinner tomorrow nite? Was i driving too fast? Too slow? What is wrong

*man? He said i was always exaggerating. Imagining things.
Always looking for trouble.*

> *Do they have children?*
> one does.
>
> *Are they married?*
> one is.
>
> *They're like you then.*
> yes.
>
> *How old are they?*
> thirty-two, thirty-three, thirty-four.
>
> *What do they do?*
> an accountant and two lawyers.
>
> *They're like you then.*
> yes.
>
> *Do they make better love than i do?*
> i'm not answering that.
>
> *Where did you meet?*
> when i traveled on the job.
>
> *Did you make love in hotels?*
> *yes.*

Did you go out together?
yes.

To bars? To movies? To restaurants?
yes.

Did you make love to them all nite?
yes.

And then got up to do your company work?
yes.

*And you fall asleep on me right after
dinner. After work. After walking the dog.*
yes.

Did you buy them things?
yes.

Did you talk on the phone with them every day?
yes.

*Do you tell them how unhappy you are
with me and the children?*
yes.

*Do you love them? Did you say that you
loved them while making love?*
i'm not answering that.

can i pull my bones
together while skeletons
come out of my head?

i am preparing for him to come home. i have exercised.
Soaked in the tub. Scrubbed my body. Oiled myself down.
What a beautiful day it's been. Warmer than usual. The
cherry blossoms on the drive are blooming prematurely. The
hibiscus are giving off a scent around the house. i have gotten
drunk off the smell. So delicate. So sweet. So loving. i have
been sleeping, no, daydreaming all day. Lounging inside my
head. i am walking up this hill. The day is green. All green.
Even the sky. i start to run down the hill and i take wing and
begin to fly and the currents turn me upside down and i be-
come young again childlike again ready to participate in all
children's games.

She's fucking my brains out. I'm so tired i just want to put
my head down at my desk. Just for a minute. What is wrong
with her? For one whole month she's turned to me every
nite. Climbed on top of me. Put my dick inside her and be-
come beautiful. Almost birdlike. She seemed to be flying as
she rode me. Arms extended. Moving from side to side. But
my God. Every night. She's fucking my brains out. I can
hardly see the morning and I'm beginning to hate the nite.

He's coming up the stairs. i've opened the venetian blinds. i love to see the trees outlined against the night air. Such beauty and space. i have oiled myself down for the night. i slept during the day. He's coming up the stairs. i have been waiting for him all day. i am singing a song i learned years ago. It is pretty like this nite. Like his eyes.

I can hardly keep my eyes open. Time to climb out of bed. Make the 7:20 train. My legs and bones hurt. i'm outta condition. Goddamn it. She's turning my way again. She's smiling. Goddamn it.

What a beautiful morning it is. i've been listening to the birds for the last couple hours. How beautifully they sing. Like sacred music. i got up and exercised while he slept. Made a cup of green tea. Oiled my body down. Climbed back into bed and began to kiss him all over . . .

Ted. Man. i'm so tired i can hardly eat this food. But i'd better eat cuz i'm losing weight. You know what man. i can't even get a hard-on when another bitch comes near me. Look at that one there with that see-through skirt on. Nothing. My dick is so limp only she can bring it up. And she does. Every nite. It ain't normal is it for a wife to fuck like she does. Is it man? It ain't normal. Like it ain't normal for a woman you've lived with for twenty years to act like this.

She was killing him. He knew it. As he approached their porch he wondered what it would be tonite. The special dinner. The erotic movie. The whirlpool. The warm oil massage until his body awakened in spite of himself. In spite of an 18-hour day at the office. As he approached the house he hesitated. He had to stay in control tonite. This was getting out of hand.

She waited for him. In the bathroom. She'd be waiting for him when he entered the shower. She'd come in to wash his back. Damn these big walk-in showers. No privacy. No time to wash yourself and dream. She'd come with those hands of hers. Soaking him. On the nipples. Chest. Then she'd travel on down to his thing. He sweet peter jesus. So tired. So forlorn. And she'd begin to tease him. Play with him. Suck him until he rose up like some fucking private first class. Anxious to do battle. And she'd watch him rise until he became Captain Sweet Peter. And she'd climb on him. Close her eyes.

honey. it's too much you know.
What?

all this sex. it's getting so i can't concentrate.
Where?

at the office. at lunch. on the train. on planes.
all i want to do is sleep.
Why?

you know why. every place i go you're there.
standing there. smiling. waiting, touching.
Yes.

in bed. i can't turn over and you're there.
lips open. smiling, all revved up.
Aren't you horny too?

yes. but enough's enough. you're my wife. it's
not normal to fuck as much as you do.
No?

it's not well, nice, to have you talk the way
you talk when we're making love.
No?

can't we go back a little, go back to our
normal life when you just wanted to sleep at
nite and make love every now and then? like me.
No.

what's wrong with you. are you having a nervous
breakdown or something?
No.

*if i become the
other woman will i be
loved like you loved her?*

*And he says i don't laugh. All this he says while he's away
in California for one week. But i've been laughing all day. All
week. All year. i know what to do now. i'll go outside and give
it away. Since he doesn't really want me. My love. My body.
When we make love his lips swell up. His legs and arms hurt.
He coughs. Drinks water. Develops a strain at his butt-hole.
Yeah. What to do now. Go outside and give it away. Pussy.
Sweet. Black pussy. For sale. Wholesale pussy. Right here.
Sweet black pussy. Hello there Mr. Mailman. What's your
name again? Oh yes. Harold. Can i call you Harry? How are
you this morning? Would you like some cold water it's so hot
out there. You want a doughnut a cookie some cereal some
sweet black pussy? Oh God. Man. Don't back away. Don't
run down the steps. Oh my God he fell. The mail is all over
the sidewalk. hee hee hee. Guess i'd better be more subtle
with the next one. hee hee hee. He's still running down the
block. Mr. Federal Express Man. Cmon over here. Let me
Fed Ex you and anyone else some Sweet Funky Pure Smell-
ing Black Pussy. hee hee hee.*

*I shall become his collector of small things; become his
collector of burps, biceps and smiles; I shall bottle his farts,
frowns and creases; I shall gather up his moans, words, out-
bursts wrap them in blue tissue paper; get to know them;
watch them grow in importance; file them in their place in
their scheme of things; I shall collect his scraps of food; ferret
them among my taste buds; allow each particle to saunter
into my cells; all aboard; calling all food particles; cmon*

board this fucking food express; climb into these sockets
golden with brine; I need to taste him again.

you can't keep his dick in your purse

Preparation for the trip to Dallas. Los Angeles. New Orleans. Baltimore. Washington. Hartford. Brownsville. (Orlando. Miami. Late check-in. Rush. Limited liability.) That's why you missed me at the airport. Hotel. Bus stop. Train station. Restaurant. (Late check-in. Rush. Limited liability.) I'm here at the justice in the eighties conference with lawyers and judges and other types advocating abbreviating orchestrating mouthing fucking spilling justice in the bars. Corridors. Bedrooms. Nothing you'd be interested in. (Luggage received damaged. Torn. Broken. Scratched. Dented. Lost.) Preparation for the trip to Chestnut Street. Market Street. Pine Street. Walnut Street. Locust Street. Lombard Street. (Early check-in. Slow and easy liability.) That's why you missed me at the office. At the office. At the office. It's a deposition. I'm deposing an entire office of women and other types needing my deposing. Nothing of interest to you. A lot of questions no answers. Long lunches. Laughter. Penises. Flirtings. Touches. Drinks. Cunts and Coke. Jazz and jacuzzis. (*Morning. Evening. Received. Damaged. Torn. Broken. Dented. Scratched. Lost.*)

I shall become a collector of me.
ishallbecomeacollectorofme.
i Shall become a collector of me.
i shall BECOME a collector of me.
I shall Become A COLLECTOR of me.
I SHALL BECOME A COLLECTOR OF ME.
ISHALLBECOMEACOLLECTOROFME.
AND PUT MEAT ON MY SOUL.

Set. No. 2

i've been keeping company, with the layaway man.
i say, i've been keeping company, with the layaway man.
each time he come by, we do it on the installment plan.

every Friday night, he comes walking up to me do'
i say, every Friday night, he comes walking up to me do'
empty pockets hanging, right on down to the floor.

gonna get me a man, who pays for it up front
i say, gonna get me a man, who pays for it up front
cuz when i needs it, can't wait til the middle of next month

i've been keeping company, with the layaway man
i say, i've been keeping company, with the layaway man
each time he come by, we do it on the installment plan
each time he come by, we do it on the installment plan

Catch the Fire

For Bill Cosby

(Sometimes I Wonder:

What to say to you now
in the soft afternoon air as you
hold us all in a single death?)

I say—

Where is your fire?

I say—

Where is your fire?

You got to find it and pass it on
You got to find it and pass it on
from you to me from me to her from her
to him from the son to the father from the
brother to the sister from the daughter to
the mother from the mother to the child.

Where is your fire? I say where is your fire?
Can't you smell it coming out of our past?
The fire of living . . . . . . Not dying
The fire of loving . . . . . . Not killing
The fire of Blackness . . . Not gangster shadows.

Where is our beautiful fire that gave light
to the world?

The fire of pyramids;
The fire that burned through the holes of
slaveships and made us breathe;
The fire that made guts into chitterlings;
The fire that took rhythms and made jazz;
The fire of sit-ins and marches that made
us jump boundaries and barriers;
The fire that took street talk and sounds
and made righteous imhotep raps.
Where is your fire, the torch of life
full of Nzingha and Nat Turner and Garvey
and Du Bois and Fannie Lou Hamer and
Martin and Malcolm and Mandela.

Sister/Sistah. Brother/Brotha. Come/Come.

CATCH YOUR FIRE. . . . . DON'T KILL
HOLD YOUR FIRE. . . . . DON'T KILL
LEARN YOUR FIRE . . . . DON'T KILL
BE THE FIRE . . . . DON'T KILL

Catch the fire and burn with eyes
that see our souls:
                WALKING.
                SINGING.
                BUILDING.
                LAUGHING.
                LEARNING.
                LOVING.
                TEACHING.
                BEING.

Hey. Brother/Brotha. Sister/Sistah.
Here is my hand.
Catch the fire . . . and live.
            live.
            livelivelivelive.
            livelivelivelive.
            live.
            live.

A Remembrance

The news of his death reached me in Trinidad around midnight. I was lecturing in the country about African-American literature and liberation, longevity and love, commitment and courage. I could not sleep. I got up and walked out of my hotel room into a night filled with stars. And I sat down in the park and talked to him. About the world. About his work. How grateful we all are that he walked on the earth, that he breathed, that he preached, that he came toward us baptizing us with his holy words. And some of us were saved because of him. Harlem man. Genius. Piercing us with his eyes and pen.

How to write of this beautiful big-eyed man who took on the country with his words? How to make anyone understand his beauty in a country that hates Blacks? How to explain his unpublished urgency? I guess I'll say that James Arthur Baldwin came out of Harlem sweating blood, counting kernel by kernel the years spent in storefront churches. I guess I'll say he walked his young steps like my grandfather, counting fatigue at the end of each day. Starved with pain, he left, came back. He questioned and answered in gold. He wept in disbelief at himself and his country and pardoned us all.

When I first read James Baldwin's *Go Tell It on the Mountain* I knew I was home: Saw my sisters and aunts and mothers and grandmothers holding up the children and churches and communities, turning their collective cheeks so that we could survive and be. And they settled down on his pages, some walking disorderly, others dressed in tunics that hid their nakedness. Ladies with no waists. Working double time with the week. Reporting daily to the Lord and their men. Saw his Black males walking sideways under an urban sky, heard their cornbread-and-sweet-potato laughter, tasted their tenement breaths as they shouted at the northern air, shouted at the hunger and bed bugs, shouted out the days with pain, and only the serum of the Lord (or liquor) could silence the anger invading their flesh.

When I first saw him on television in the early sixties, I felt immediately a kinship with this man whose anger and disappointment with America's contradictions trans-formed his face into a warrior's face, whose tongue trans-formed our massacres into triumphs. And he left behind a hundred TV deaths: scholars, writers, teachers, and jour-nalists shipwrecked by his revivals and sermons. And the Black audiences watched and shouted amen and felt clean and conscious and chosen.

When I first met him in the late sixties, I was stricken by his smile smiling out at the New York City audience he had just attacked. I was transfixed by his hands and voice bat-tling each other for space as they pierced, caressed, and challenged the crowded auditorium. I rushed toward the stage after the talking was done, I rushed toward the stage to touch his hands, for I knew those hands could heal me, could heal us all because his starting place had been the altar of the Lord. His starting place had been an America that had genuflected over Black bones. Now those bones were rattling discontent and pulling themselves upright in an unrighteous land. And Jimmy Baldwin's mouth, traveling like a fire in the wind, gave us the songs, the marrow and the speech as we began our hesitant, turbulent and insistent walk against surrogates and sheriffs, governors and goons, patriarchs and patriots, missionaries and 'ministrators of the status quo.

I was too shy too scared too much a stutterer to say much of anything to him that night. I managed to say a hello and a few thank-you's as I ran out of the auditorium back to a Riverside Drive apartment, as I carried his resident spirit through the coming nights, as I began to integrate his fire into my speech. No longer slavery-bound. No longer Negro-bound. No longer ugly or scared. But terrifyingly beautiful as I, we, began to celebrate the sixties and seventies. Opening and shutting with martyrs. A million bodies coming and going. Shaking off old fears. Laughing. Weeping. Hoping. Studying. Trying to make a colony finally into a country. Responsible to all its citizens. I knew finally as the Scriptures know that "the things that have been done in the dark will be known on the housetops."

The last time I saw Jimmy Baldwin was at Cornell University. But it is not of that time that I want to speak, but of the next to the last time we spoke in Atlanta. An Atlanta coming out from under serial murders. An Atlanta that looked on him as an outsider attempting to stir up things better left unsaid.

A magazine editor motioned to me as I entered the hotel lobby at midnight, eyes heading straight for my room, head tired from a day of judging plays. He took me to the table where Jimmy was holding court. Elder statesman. Journeying toward himself. Testifying with his hand and mouth about his meeting with professors and politicians and preachers. He had listened to activists and soothsayers and students for days, and his hands shook from the colors of the night, and the sound of fear fell close to his ears each day.

We parted at five o'clock in the morning. I had seen Atlanta through his eyes, and I knew as he knew that the country had abandoned reason. But he stayed in Atlanta and continued to do his duty to the country. Raising the consciousness of a city. And the world.

I was out of town, traveling in the Midwest on flat lands with no curves, the last time he visited Philadelphia. He had come to speak with poet Gwendolyn Brooks at the Afro-American Historical and Cultural Museum. One of my twins, Mungu, walked up to Jimmy that night, shook his hand and heard his male laughter as he introduced himself. They hugged each other, then my son listened to his Baldwinian talk cast aside the commotion of the night. The next day Mungu greeted me with Jimmy's sounds, and he and his brother Morani thanked me for insisting that they travel to the museum to hear Mr. Baldwin and Ms. Brooks.

Today, home from Trinidad, I thank James Arthur Baldwin for his legacy of fire. A fine rain of words when we had no tongues. He set fire to our eyes. Made a single look, gesture endure. Made a people meaningful and moral. Responsible finally for all our sweet and terrible lives.

Poem for July 4, 1994

For President Václav Havel

I.

It is essential that Summer be grafted to
bones marrow earth clouds blood the
eyes of our ancestors.
It is essential to smell the beginning
words where Washington, Madison, Hamilton,
Adams, Jefferson assembled amid cries of:

> "The people lack of information"
> "We grow more and more skeptical"
> "This Constitution is a triple-headed monster"
> "Blacks are property"

It is essential to remember how cold the sun
how warm the snow snapping
around the ragged feet of soldiers and slaves.
It is essential to string the sky
with the saliva of Slavs and
Germans and Anglos and French
and Italians and Scandinavians,
and Spaniards and Mexicans and Poles
and Africans and Native Americans.
It is essential that we always repeat:
> we the people,
> we the people,
> we the people.

2.

"Let us go into the fields" one
brother told the other brother. And
the sound of exact death
raising tombs across the centuries.
Across the oceans. Across the land.

3.

It is essential that we finally understand:
this is the time for the creative
human being
the human being who decides
to walk upright in a human
fashion in order to save this
earth from extinction.

This is the time for the creative
Man. Woman. Who must decide
that She. He. Can live in peace.
Racial and sexual justice on
this earth.

This is the time for you and me.
African American. Whites. Latinos.
Gays. Asians. Jews. Native
Americans. Lesbians. Muslims.
All of us must finally bury
the elitism of race superiority
the elitism of sexual superiority
the elitism of economic superiority
the elitism of religious superiority.

So we welcome you on the celebration
of 218 years Philadelphia. America.

So we salute you and say:
Come, come, come, move out into this world
nourish your lives with a
spirituality that allows us to respect
each other's birth.
come, come, come, nourish the world where
every 3 days 120,000 children die
of starvation or the effects of starvation;
come, come, come, nourish the world
where we will no longer hear the
screams and cries of women, girls,
and children in Bosnia, El Salvador,
Rwanda . . . AhAhAhAh AHAHAHHHHH

Ma-ma. Dada. Mamacita. Baba.
Mama. Papa. Momma. Poppi.
The soldiers are marching in the streets
near the hospital but the nurses say
we are safe and the soldiers are
laughing marching firing calling
out to us i don't want to die i
am only 9 yrs old, i am only 10 yrs old
i am only 11 yrs old and i cannot
get out of the bed because they have cut
off one of my legs and i hear the soldiers
coming toward our rooms and i hear
the screams and the children are
running out of the room i can't get out
of the bed i don't want to die Don't
let me die Rwanda. America. United
Nations. Don't let me die . . . .

And if we nourish ourselves, our communities
our countries and say

     no more hiroshima
     no more auschwitz
     no more wounded knee
     no more middle passage
     no more slavery
     no more Bosnia
     no more Rwanda

No more intoxicating ideas of
racial superiority
as we walk toward abundance
we will never forget

> the earth
> the sea
> the children
> the people

For *we the people* will always be arriving
a ceremony of thunder
waking up the earth
opening our eyes to human
monuments.
    And it'll get better
    it'll get better
if *we the people* work, organize, resist,
come together for peace, racial, social
and sexual justice
    it'll get better
    it'll get better.

This Is Not a Small Voice

This is not a small voice
you hear   this is a large
voice coming out of these cities.
This is the voice of LaTanya.
Kadesha. Shaniqua. This
is the voice of Antoine.
Darryl. Shaquille.
Running over waters
navigating the hallways
of our schools spilling out
on the corners of our cities and
no epitaphs spill out of their river mouths.

This is not a small love
you hear   this is a large
love, a passion for kissing learning
on its face.
This is a love that crowns the feet with hands
that nourishes, conceives, feels the water sails
mends the children,
folds them inside our history where they
toast more than the flesh
where they suck the bones of the alphabet
and spit out closed vowels.
This is a love colored with iron and lace.
This is a love initialed Black Genius.

This is not a small voice
you hear.

Like

Listening to the News

Like

All i did was
go down on him
in the middle of
the dance floor
cuz he is a movie
star he is a blk/
man "live" rt off
the screen fulfilling
my wildest dreams.

Like.

Yeah. All i did
was suck him in tune
to *that's the way love goes*
while boogeying feet
stunning thighs pressed
together in rhythm cuz he
wanted it and i wanted
to be seen with him
cuz he's in the movies on the
big screen bigger than life
bigger than all of my
hollywood dreams
cuz see

i need to have my say
among all the unsaid
lives i deal with.

Like.
Yeah.

Haiku 1

i have died and dreamed
myself back to your arms where
what i died for sleeps.

Haiku 9

the sprawling sound
of my death sails on the wind
a white butterfly.

V *from*

DOES YOUR HOUSE
HAVE LIONS?
1997

FATHER'S VOICE

the day he traveled to my daughter's house
it was june. he cursed me with his morning nod
of anger as he filtered his callous
walk. skip. hop. feet slipshod
from 125th street bars, face curled with odd
reflections. the skin of a father is accented
in the sentence of the unaccented.

i was a southern Negro man playing music
married to a high yellow woman who loved my unheard
face, who slept with me in nordic
beauty. i prisoner since my birth to fear
i unfashioned buried in an open grave
of mornings unclapped with constant sight
of masters fattened decked with my diminished light.

this love. this first wife of mine, died in childbirth
this face of complex lace exiled her breath
into another design, and i died became wanderlust
demanded recompense from friends for my heartbreak
cursed the land for this new heartache
put her away with a youthful pause
never called her name again, wrapped my heart in gauze.

became romeo bound, applauded women
as i squeezed their syrup, drank their stenciled
face, danced between their legs, placed my swollen
shank to the world, became man distilled
early twentieth-century black man fossilled
fulfilled by women things, foreclosing on my life.
mother where do i go before i arrive?

she wasn't as beautiful as my first wife
this ruby-colored girl insinuating her limb
against my thigh positioning her wild-life
her non-virginal smell as virginal her climb
towards me with slow walking heels made me limp
made me stumble, made my legs squint
until i stopped, stepped inside her footprint.

i did not want to leave you son, this flame
this pecan-colored festival requested me
not my child, your sister. your mother could not frame
herself as her mother and i absentee
father, and i nightclub owner carefree
did not heed her blood, did not see my girl's eyes
shaved buckled down with southern thighs.

now my seventy-eight years urge me on your land
now my predator legs prey, broadcast
no new nightmares no longer birdman
of cornerstone comes, i come to collapse the past
while bonfires burn up your orphan's mask
i sing a dirge of lost black southern manhood
this harlem man begging pardon, secreting old.

i was told i don't remember who
i think i was told he entered his sister's house
cursed me anew, tried to tattoo
her tongue with worms, tried to arouse
her slumbering veins to espouse
his venom and she leaned slapped him still
stilled his mouth across early morning chill.

rumor has it that he slapped her hard
down purgatorial sounds of caress
rumor has it that he rushed her down a boulevard
of mad laughter while his hands grabbed harness—
like her arms and she, avenger and she heiress
to naked lightning, detonated him, began her dance
of looted hems gathering together for his inheritance.

blood the sound of blood paddling down the road
blood the taste of blood choking their eyes
and my son's body blood-stained red
with country-lies, city-lies, father-lies, mother-lies,
and my daughter clamoring to exorcise
old thieves trespassing in an old refrain
conjured up a blue-black chord to ordain.

wa ma ne ho mene so oo
oseee yei, oseee yei, oseee yei
wa ma ne ho mene so oo
he has become holy as he walks toward daresay
can you hear his blood tissue ready to pray
he who wore death discourages any plague
he who was an orphan now recollects his legs.

wa ma ne ho mene so oo: he is arising in all his majesty
oseee yei: a shout of praise

VI

from

LIKE THE SINGING COMING OFF THE DRUMS

Love Poems
1998

Dancing

i dreamt i was tangoing with
you, you held me so close
we were like the singing coming off the drums.
you made me squeeze muscles
lean back on the sound
of corpuscles sliding in blood.
i heard my thighs singing.

Haiku

(for you)

love between us is
speech and breath. loving you is
a long river running.

Tanka

i thought about you
the pain of not having
you cruising my bones.
no morning saliva smiles this
frantic fugue about no you.

Blues Haiku

let me be yo wil
derness let me be yo wind
blowing you all day.

Blues Haiku

am i yo philly
outpost? man when you sail in
to my house, you docked.

Haiku

my womb is a dance
of leaves sweating swift winds
i laugh with guitars.

Love Poem

(for Tupac)

1.

we smell the
wounds hear the
red vowels
from your tongue.

the old ones
say we don't
die we are
just passing
through into
another space.

i say they
have tried to
cut out your
heart and eat
it slowly.

we stretch our
ears to hear
your blood young
warrior.

2.

where are your fathers?
i see your mothers gathering
around your wounds folding
your arms shutting your
eyes wrapping you in prayer.

where are the fathers?
zootsuited eyes dancing
their days away.
what have they taught you
about power and peace.

where are the fathers
strutting their furlined
intellect bowing their
faces in the crotch
of academia and corporations
burying their tongues
in lunchtime pink
and black pussies
where are the fathers to teach
beyond stayinschooluse
acondomstrikewhilethe
iron'shotkeephopealive.
where have the fathers buried their voices?

3.

whose gold is carrying you home?
whose wealth is walking you through
this urban terror? whose greed
left you shipwrecked with golden
eyes staring in sudden death?

4.

you were in
a place hot
at the edge
of our minds.
you were in
a new world
a country
pushing with
blk corpses
distinct with
paleness and
it swallowed
you whole.

5.

i will not
burp you up.
i hold you
close to my heart.

VII

NEW
WORKS

Mrs. Benita Jones Speaks

Why?

You asking me why I'm moving. You reporters are something else you know. Why do you think? I was gonna tough it out. Thought all of this commotion would die down. Thought the people living here could understand a woman, a mother wanting to give her children a better life. Look. All I'm looking for is a nice house for my kids. A safe place to bring them up.

What?

What do I think about my neighbors? These people. These people who have sprayed the word *nigger* on my door. These people who finally threatened my children. My children did you hear me? Have you ever held a child in your arms while she shook her insides out? She was so scared I cried her to sleep. How do you ever tell a child again that she's safe? Huh?

What do I think of these people? Huh? What should anyone think? What should you reporters think? What should the city think? What should the mayor think? What should the country think?

A woman came to my door yesterday and said these people here wasn't bad. They was just concerned about their neighborhood. They had worked so hard so they didn't want it messed up with people who didn't know what it meant to live in a decent neighborhood. She said they keep their neighborhood clean. She said they had no crime in their streets. She said they keep their houses clean. She said they keep their children clean. She said they keep themselves clean. She said there were no bad guys here. Just people protecting their neighborhood and property.

Huh? Did she say clean? Clean? You wanna see clean? Do you wanna see my floors? They so clean you could eat offa them. And I scrub my children. I scrub them every day. Hard. So hard that some of the black almost come offa them. But it don't you know. Hee hee.

What do you guys want me to do? Huh? Call them names too? My God won't let me do that. My God won't let me become indecent like them. My God. . . . And I don't know how their God can let them do what they do.

What do you guys think about her saying "There ain't no bad guys here"? Am I the bad guy for wanting to move into a place I can afford? Am I the bad guy for being black and female and a single woman with three children? Am I the bad guy because I don't look like them?

What do you think? They look like y'all. You know they could be your mommas and fathers. Your sisters and brothers. You know. But you know what I really can't figure out? It's their eyes. I can't figure out what to make about their eyes and mouths so framed with hatred. Their tongues full of worms you know. Their bodies anxious to do damage to children's eyes. Their hands poised to paint obscenities; their thumbs curled to hurl stones at my windows.

Huh?

What am I gonna do? What am I gonna do? I'm gonna

move in with my mama. She lives in Mt. Airy. I'll probably stay with her for a while. Try to figure out where else to go. Where else I can live. What do you think I should do? Huh? You got a house in your neighborhood I can move into? You got a house for a respectable hard-working, underpaid black woman who can buy a house on her own?

Me. This Black woman. Staring out at you. You got a neighborhood for her and her three kids? With furniture paid for. With clothes paid for. With a decent job that pays the mortgage and utilities and a few bills. Not enough money for a car payment. But we manage.

Answer me. Where does a Black woman go when she is me, trailed by myths that this country has invented about her? Where to go to, when all of you have been there already, and claimed the turf as your own and you watch the rest of us shipwrecked by circumstance and color, looking. Waiting. Needing.

What?

Am I angry? Angry? About this? Are you angry about this? No. I am surprised again. I am surprised that the good folks in Philadelphia and the country would continue to allow this to happen. I am concerned that my children have seen other children look at 'em like they was dirt. I am alarmed that people didn't come out in a peace vigil. That the Christians didn't come out in a Christian vigil. That the educators did not come out to educate. That the athletes did not come to play the real game. I am amazed that God disappeared from their eyes. That God disappeared again in this city with so many churches. So many schools. So many people wanting just to be clean in their own neighborhood.

Morning Song and Evening Walk

1.

Tonite in need of you
and God
I move imperfect
through this ancient city.

Quiet. No one hears
No one feels the tears
of multitudes.

The silence thickens
I have lost the shore
of your kind seasons
who will hear my voice
nasal against distinguished
actors.

O I am tired
of voices without sound
I will rest on this ground
full of mass hymns.

2.

You have been here since I can remember Martin
from Selma to Montgomery from Watts to Chicago

from Nobel Peace Prize to Memphis, Tennessee.
Unmoved among the angles and corners
of aristocratic confusion.

It was a time to be born
forced forward a time
to wander inside drums
the good times with eyes like stars
and soldiers without medals or weapons
but honor, yes.

And you told us: *the storm is rising against the*
privileged minority of the earth, from which there is no
shelter in isolation or armament
and you told us: the storm will
not abate until a just distribution of the fruits of
the earth enables men (and women) everywhere to live
in dignity and human decency.

3.

All summerlong it has rained
and the water rises in our throats
and all that we sing is rumored
forgotten.
Whom shall we call when this song comes of age?

And they came into the city carrying their fastings
in their eyes and the young 9-year-old Sudanese
boy said, "I want something to eat at nite a
place to sleep."
And they came into the city hands salivating guns,
and the young 9-year-old words snapped red
with vowels:
Mama mama Auntie auntie I dead I dead I deaddddd.

4.

In our city of lost alphabets
where only our eyes strengthen the children
you spoke like Peter like John
you fisherman of tongues
untangling our wings
you inaugurated iron for our masks
exiled no one with your touch
and we felt the thunder in your hands.

We are soldiers in the army
we have to fight, although we have to cry.
We have to hold up the freedom banners
we have to hold it up until we die.

And you said we must keep going and we became
small miracles, pushed the wind down, entered

the slow bloodstream of America
surrounded streets and "reconcentradas," tuned
our legs against Olympic politicians elaborate cadavers
growing fat underneath western hats.
And we scraped the rust from old laws
went floor by floor window by window
and clean faces rose from the dust
became new brides and bridegrooms among change
men and women coming for their inheritance.
And you challenged us to catch up with our
own breaths to breathe in Latinos Asians Native Americans
Whites Blacks Gays Lesbians Muslims and Jews, to gather
up our rainbow-colored skins in peace and racial justice
as we try to answer your long-ago question: Is there
a nonviolent peacemaking army that can shut down
the Pentagon?

And you challenged us to breathe in Bernard Haring's words:
the materialistic growth—mania for
more and more production and more
and more markets for selling unnecessary
and even damaging products is a
sin against the generation to come
what shall we leave to them:
rubbish, atomic weapons numerous
enough to make the earth
uninhabitable, a poisoned
atmosphere, polluted water?

5.

"Love in practice is a harsh and dreadful
thing compared to love in dreams," said a Russian writer.
Now I know at great cost Martin that as we burn
something moves out of the flames
(call it spirit or apparition)
till no fire or body or ash remain
we breathe out and smell the world again
Aye-Aye-Aye Ayo-Ayo-Ayo Ayeee-Ayeee-Ayeee
Amen men men men Awoman woman woman woman
Men men men Woman woman woman
Men men Woman woman
Men Woman
Womanmen.

For Sweet Honey in the Rock

I'm gonna stay on the battlefield
I'm gonna stay on the battlefield
I'm gonna stay on the battlefield til I die.

I'm gonna stay on the battlefield
I'm gonna stay on the battlefield
I'm gonna stay on the battlefield til I die.

i had come into the city carrying life in my eyes
amid rumors of death,
calling out to everyone who would listen
it is time to move us all into another century
time for freedom and racial and sexual justice
time for women and children and men time for hands unbound
i had come into the city wearing peaceful breasts
and the spaces between us smiled
i had come into the city carrying life in my eyes.
i had come into the city carrying life in my eyes.

And they followed us in their cars with their computers
and their tongues crawled with caterpillars
and they bumped us off the road turned over our cars,
and they bombed our buildings killed our babies,
and they shot our doctors maintaining our bodies,
and their courts changed into confessionals
but we kept on organizing we kept on teaching believing
loving doing what was holy moving to a higher ground

even though our hands were full of slaughtered teeth
but we held out our eyes delirious with grace.
but we held out our eyes delirious with grace.

I'm gonna treat everybody right
I'm gonna treat everybody right
I'm gonna treat everybody right til I die.

I'm gonna treat everybody right
I'm gonna treat everybody right
I'm gonna treat everybody right til I die.

come. i say come, you sitting still in domestic bacteria
come. i say come, you standing still in double-breasted mornings
come. i say come, and return to the fight.
this fight for the earth
this fight for our children
this fight for our life
we need your hurricane voices
we need your sacred hands

i say, come, sister, brother to the battlefield
come into the rain forests
come into the hood
come into the barrio
come into the schools
come into the abortion clinics

come into the prisons
come and caress our spines

i say come, wrap your feet around justice
i say come, wrap your tongues around truth
i say come, wrap your hands with deeds and prayer
you brown ones
you yellow ones
you black ones
you gay ones
you white ones
you lesbian ones

Comecomecomecomecome to this battlefield
called life, called life, called life. . . .

I'm gonna stay on the battlefield
I'm gonna stay on the battlefield
I'm gonna stay on the battlefield til I die.

I'm gonna stay on the battlefield
I'm gonna stay on the battlefield
I'm gonna stay on the battlefield til I die.

Aaaayeee Babo (Praise God)

1.

There are women sailing the sky
I walk between them
They who wear silk, muslin and burlap skins touching mine
They who dance between urine and violets
They who are soiled disinherited angels with masculine eyes.

This earth is hard symmetry
This earth of feverish war
This earth inflamed with hate
This patch of tongues corroding the earth's air.
Who will journey to the place we require of humans?
I grow thin on these algebraic equations reduced to a final
    common denominator.

2.

I turn away from funerals from morning lightning
I feast on rain and laughter
What is this sound I hear moving through our bones
I breathe out leaving our scent in the air.

3.

I came to this life with serious hands
I came observing the terrorist eyes moving in and out of
    Southern corners
I wanted to be the color of bells
I wanted to surround trees and spill autumn from my fingers
I came to this life with serious feet—heard other footsteps
    gathering around me
Women whose bodies exploded with flowers.

4.

Life.
Life is
from curled embryo
to greed
to flesh
transistors
webpages obscuring butterflies.

Our life
is a feast of flutes
orbiting chapels
no beggar women here
no treasonous spirit here
just a praise touch

created from our spirit tongues
We bring the noise of mountain language
We bring the noise of Sunday mansions
We enter together paddling a river of risks
in order to reshape This wind, This sea,
This sky, This dungeon of syllables
We have become nightingales singing us out of fear
Splashing the failed places with light.

We are here.
On the green of leaves
On the shifting waves of blues,
Knowing once that our places divided us
Knowing once that our color divided us
Knowing once that our class divided us
Knowing once that our sex divided us
Knowing once that our country divided us
Now we carry the signature of women in our veins
Now we build our reconciliation canes in morning fields
Now the days no longer betray us
and we ascend into wave after wave of our blood milk.
What can we say without blood?

5.

Her Story.
Herstory smiles at us.

Little by little we shall interpret the decorum of peace
Little by little we shall make circles of these triangular stars
We Shall strip-mine the world's eyes of secrets
We shall gather up our voices
Braid them into our flesh like emeralds
Come. Bring us all the women's hands
Let us knead calluses into smiles
Let us gather the mountains in our children's eyes
Distill our unawakened love
Say hello to the mangoes
   the uninformed men
   the nuns
   the prostitutes
   the rainmothers
   the squirrels
   the clouds
   the homeless.
Come. Celebrate our footsteps insatiable as sudden breathing
Love curves the journey of these women sails
Love says Awoman. Awoman to these tongues of thunder

Come celebrate this prayer
I bring to our common ground.
It is enough
to confound the conquistadores
it is enough to shape our lace,
our name.

Make us become healers
Come celebrate the poor
the women
the gays
the lesbians
the men
the children
the black, brown, yellow, white
Sweat peeling with stories

Aaaaayeee babo.
I spit on the ground
I spit language on the dust
I spit memory on the water
I spit hope on this seminary
I spit teeth on the wonder of women, holy volcanic women
Recapturing the memory of our most sacred sounds.

Come
where the drum speaks
come tongued by fire and water and bone
come praise God and
Ogun and Shango and
Olukun and Oya and
Jesus
Come praise our innocence
our decision to be human

reenter the spirit of morning doves
and our God is near
I say our God is near
I say our God is near
Aaaayeee babo Aaaayeee babo Aaaayeee babo
(Praise God).

CREDITS